ENNEAGRAM
TRANSFORMATIONS

*The definitive text of
Enneagram theory and descriptions.*
PERSONALITY TYPES
Using the Enneagram for Self-Discovery   1987

Practical applications of the Enneagram in your life.
UNDERSTANDING THE ENNEAGRAM
The Practical Guide to Personality Types   1990

*An introduction to the Enneagram
with an accurate personality test.*
DISCOVERING YOUR
PERSONALITY TYPE
The Enneagram Questionnaire   1992

Spiritual and psychological help for each type.
ENNEAGRAM TRANSFORMATIONS
*Releases and Affirmations for Healing
Your Personality Type*   1993

Forthcoming in 1994
Using the Enneagram for personal growth.
WORKING WITH THE ENNEAGRAM
Transforming the Personality Types

ENNEAGRAM TRANSFORMATIONS

Releases and Affirmations for Healing Your Personality Type

Don Richard Riso

HOUGHTON MIFFLIN COMPANY

Boston · New York

1993

Library of Congress Cataloging-in-Publication Data

Riso, Don Richard.
   Enneagram transformations : releases and affirmations for healing your personality type / Don Richard Riso.
        p.   cm.
   ISBN 0-395-65786-5 (pbk.)
   1. Enneagram—Problems, exercises, etc.   2. Personality change—Problems, exercises, etc.   3. Affirmations.
   I. Title.
   BF698.35.E54R57
   155.2′6—dc20   92-28727
                              CIP

Printed in the United States of America

BP   10   9   8   7   6   5   4   3   2

Line drawings by Mark Desveaux

Based on a book design by Joyce C. Weston

For

BETTE

Contents

Acknowledgments

Readers and colleagues have been asking where I get my material, especially since my books have been appearing rather rapidly now. There are several answers to that question, although they can probably be reduced to two. First, the world, and especially people, are endless sources of material for Enneagram books — once one learns to see the types correctly. An extraordinary amount of knowledge can be had by noticing what is "right under your nose." The hardest part is, of course, to put one's preconceptions aside to observe real people in the real world. But if one does so, the material seems to present itself. All one has to do is write it down.

Ideas for Enneagram books have also been suggested by my students, and this particular book, *Enneagram Transformations*, is a case in point. George Kwast, a graduate of my Trainings, suggested that I write affirmations for each personality type that could be read in times of crisis. George felt that it would be useful if I provided readers with a tool they could use when they were anxious, under stress, or otherwise in danger of spiraling down the Levels of Development into unhealthy states. He also felt that if people were already in a crisis, and feeling threatened and imbalanced, affirmations would be a helpful way of moving them out of their painful state. I have taken George's suggestion, and the result is this book. I am indebted to him, as is anyone who benefits from these Transformations.

I am equally in debt to my editor at Houghton Mifflin, Ruth Hapgood. The birth of this book was so sudden that it was as much a surprise to me as it was to my publisher, Houghton Mifflin. When I presented Ruth with the manuscript, her enthusiasm was extremely encouraging. She also wanted the book to be published promptly so that readers could benefit from the Transformations. Without Ruth's support, this book could not have been made available so quickly.

The warmth and professionalism of Sue Tecce, Ruth's editorial assistant, is also greatly appreciated. Phone calls flew between New York and Boston as we shaped the manuscript, and Sue was on top of every situation with her usual thoroughness and thoughtfulness. Dorothy Paschal, the manuscript editor, helped me bring more clarity and simplicity to the book.

Other students have also contributed in various ways. Barbara Hribar wrote her own Enneagram affirmations at my first Professional Training in 1990, thus inspiring George and planting the seed for this book. Colleen McDonald advised me about using affirmations, as did Betsey Bittlingmaier, Ph.D., who also field-tested them with her therapy groups. Phyllis Houck Cloninger and Linda Donohue also encouraged me with this project. Brian Taylor has continued to supply shrewd good sense and valuable advice at every turn, as have Bradshaw and Digby. They all have my affectionate and heartfelt thanks.

My assistant, Russ Hudson, has, in terms of the actual writing of this book, contributed more than anyone else. Russ urged me to get "inside" each of the types more deeply, and he continued to press me until we both felt that we had done so. I say "we" because the Transformations reflect our ongoing collaboration about the Enneagram. He is in a very true sense the co-author of this book. However helpful you feel the Transformations are, they would not have been nearly so without his many suggestions and contributions. Would that every writer had an assistant as dedicated and talented as Russ.

PART I

Releasing Our Pain,
Affirming Our Strength

Transformation
and the Enneagram

These Transformations (as I have named the Releases and Affirmations for each personality type) are but one answer to the often asked question of students new to the Enneagram,* "Now that I know my type, what can I do with it?"

One important answer is that knowing our type helps us become more conscious self-observers, and self-observation is necessary if we are to become free of our unthinking, mechanical reactions. If we do not observe ourselves, we cannot ever hope to be our own master. We will be like marionettes yanked by every impulse tugging on our strings.

If we learn to observe ourselves, however, we create the possibility of consciously choosing our behavior, and thereby of living more effectively. To do this, we must learn how *not* to identify with our personality — and this is where the Enneagram can be extremely valuable. Paradoxically, we need to see our personality in operation before we can learn how not to identify with it. We must experience the process of disidentifying with our personality and its habitual responses many times before we can

---

* Pronounced ANY-a-gram.

acquire a "taste" for nonidentification and thus become convinced of its worthwhile results in our lives.

If we observe ourselves carefully, we will discover that most of what goes on in us is the constant churning of our mechanical responses, little more than the machinery of our personality grinding along pretty much on its own. We find that our attention is constantly possessed by ever-changing fears and desires, fantasies and associations, that lead nowhere while keeping us out of touch with our deeper self. Ironically, we build our identity out of these chaotic and unconscious impulses — embracing them as our self, and defending them with our life.

Ideas about observing ourselves, learning how not to identify with our personality, and of practicing nonidentification with our ego sound foreign and are rather threatening to most of us. And yet, if we think about it, we can probably recall moments of spontaneous nonidentification: most of us have experienced times when we were free from our personality and its (usually negative) responses. Sometimes a life-threatening crisis brings such a moment; sometimes an act of selfless love, an experience of the grandeur of nature, or an encounter with death "wakes us up" to something deep in us that is not our personality and is also clearly not the product of our ego. Moments such as these are vivid and profoundly liberating. Looking back on them, we usually regard them as the times when we were most alive.

An important part of our spiritual quest, then, becomes learning to have moments such as these more often. We need to find a way of waking up and of being more present to our own lives so that they can happen more frequently. There is no better tool than the Enneagram to help us observe ourselves, and thereby get some "distance" on our personality. The more we look into it, the more we will discover that getting distance on our personality is a very good thing indeed. When we learn to disidentify with our personality, instead of feeling naked and deprived, we find that our personality is actually what has blocked us most of our lives. Rather than having been our ally, our personality has been our secret enemy; rather than help us live more effectively, it has gotten in our way; rather than make us stronger, it has made us weaker and more afraid.

The way to escape from the grip of personality is to create a "gap" between our inner-observer and our personality. At first, this gap may last only a second between a stimulus and our response. Our attention will become occupied almost immediately with our personality's usual associations. But we will have also experienced something new. In the brief gap that we have created, we catch a glimpse of a deeper, more essential self and the possibility of real freedom.

Of course, none of this is easy, and the effort to not identify with our ego must be made over and over again. Freedom and real consciousness are won by constantly struggling with all of the reactive, automatic forces at work in us. We must struggle especially with that dark force in us that does not want us to be free or aware of anything higher in ourselves. Part of us wants us to remain asleep, in flight from being, and gladly prevents us from realizing that something more is within our reach.

The Enneagram can help us deal with the contrary forces of our personality by naming them and releasing them. Seeing ourselves and letting go of what is seducing us away from a fuller, more authentic life is at the heart of our daily struggle. This is a difficult and subtle task, and we need the wisdom of the Enneagram to undertake it.

These Transformations are different from those usually found in self-help books. They represent a new approach to self-help, and are the latest development of my interpretation of the Enneagram.

Releases and Affirmations help us "reprogram" our behavior by healing the way we think about ourselves. The Releases allow us first to acknowledge the emotional problems under which we labor. They give us a chance to name the sources of pain in our lives and to work through our negative issues so that we can let them go. They take us "inside" our type to touch the pain that lies at the root of our problems, allowing us to overcome resistance, denial, and self-deception. Naturally, by acknowledging the negative aspects of our personality, we do not want to reinforce them in any way. But we do want to "make the unconscious conscious" by shining a light on our hidden conflicts and contradictions.

In the Affirmations for each type, we turn to the positive qualities that need to be affirmed. As we have just seen, when we release negative attitudes, we let go of a damaged and painful part of us from our past that is causing us problems in the present. When we affirm something good about ourselves, we replace those old, negative beliefs with new, positive ones. The saying "Nature abhors a vacuum" is true of the mind as well, for the mind also needs to be filled. Once a negative attitude has been released, we need to replace it with a positive one; otherwise, the negative message will come rushing back.

The Enneagram thus provides us with two "missing pieces" that are essential for our growth. Since different personality types are *different*, treating all people as if they were alike undermines the benefits that could be obtained by many self-help programs. The Enneagram adds important specificity to our quest for growth. Specificity is necessary because sound advice for one type may not be sound advice for another. Generalizations about how people grow, how they develop good relationships, or how they can be better friends or parents — among a host of things — either fall flat or can be dangerous if differences between personality types are not taken into account. The Enneagram helps us recognize that each personality type is the filter that affects all of our spiritual and psychological growth. Learning to heal one's type — to make that filter more accessible and less distorting — is the first step on any spiritual or personal quest.

The second way the Enneagram can be useful for

self-transformation is by taking into account the internal Levels of Development of each type. The Releases and Affirmations work by following the Levels "from the bottom up" — beginning with the negative roots of each type's unhappiness and moving upward through the Levels toward health and balance.

The Levels of Development are a measure of our state of being, ranging from extremely unhealthy states to highly integrated and balanced ones. Each of us moves up and down the Levels of our type according to the habits and defenses that have taken root in us. Understanding the Levels is immensely valuable for growth since, more than any other factor, they show us what we will encounter on the way toward either health or neurosis. The Levels of Development mark the milestones on our journey, and to know them is to have a way of measuring where we have come from and where we are going.

As we move through the Levels, our state of being changes as we release what needs to be released and affirm what needs to be affirmed. As the negative changes into the positive and we begin to sense higher possibilities for ourselves, the Affirmations become prayers from the heart in which we finally do find healing.

A Brief Introduction
to the Enneagram

Rather than explain how the Enneagram works in detail, let me refer new readers to my other books, *Personality Types* (1987), *Understanding the Enneagram* (1990), and *Discovering Your Personality Type* (1992).*

My first book, *Personality Types*, contains the only systematic descriptions of the types available, including descriptions of the Directions of Integration and Disintegration and the wings for each type. It is recommended for those who want to have an in-depth treatment of this system. My second book, *Understanding the Enneagram*, contains all-new

---

* Other books on the Enneagram are also available. Readers have become confused, however, by the contradictions among them. In my opinion, serious inaccuracies have resulted because some authors have not undertaken a detailed critical examination of the older Enneagram material that they were taught. Books on relationships, spirituality, or business, for that matter, will be of little use if they are based on distorted or erroneous notions of the types. Those interested in the Enneagram are urged to read all of the Enneagram books critically, to think for themselves, and always to judge everything by their own experience. If an interpretation or application of the Enneagram does not clarify your own experience of people in the real world, it is not only relatively worthless, it is potentially dangerous.

material and is a brief guide that answers questions about how to apply the Enneagram in your daily life. *Discovering Your Personality Type,* the shortest of the three, contains a randomized questionnaire (the *Riso Enneagram Type Indicator* or RETI) to help identify your personality type and extensive materials to help you interpret the results.

The following brief discussion is included to introduce the Enneagram to those who are new to this simple, yet ultimately complex, typology. It presents only the ideas that are necessary for you to use the Releases and Affirmations effectively.

Identifying Your Basic Personality Type

Each of us has a primary role that we play in life. Which of the following nine roles fits you best most of the time?

The Peacemaker

9

The Leader 8   1 The Reformer

The Generalist 7   2 The Helper

The Loyalist 6   3 The Motivator

The Thinker 5   4 The Artist

The Riso Enneagram Type Names

A wide range of behaviors and motivations is associated with each of these roles. The following are four key behaviors for each personality type; they are merely highlights and do not represent the full spectrum found in each. See if the type you have tentatively chosen still seems accurate.

The *One, the Reformer,* is rational, principled, orderly, and self-righteous.

The *Two, the Helper,* is caring, generous, possessive, and manipulative.

The *Three, the Motivator,* is adaptable, ambitious, image-oriented, and hostile.

The *Four, the Artist,* is intuitive, individualistic, self-absorbed, and depressive.

The *Five, the Thinker,* is perceptive, original, provocative, and eccentric.

The *Six, the Loyalist,* is engaging, responsible, defensive, and anxious.

The *Seven, the Generalist,* is enthusiastic, accomplished, excessive, and manic.

The *Eight, the Leader,* is self-confident, decisive, dominating, and combative.

The *Nine, the Peacemaker,* is receptive, optimistic, complacent, and disengaged.

Although you may still not be certain of your type after reading these short descriptions, you probably have narrowed down the possibilities to two or three. If the informal Forewords found at the beginning of each set of Transformations and, more important, the Releases and Affirmations themselves hit home, your "diagnosis" of your basic personality type is most likely on the right track. Keep an open mind about this, however, until you have read the full descriptions in my other books, or have taken the diagnostic questionnaire (RETI) in *Discovering Your Personality Type.*

The Wing

Experience tells us that no one is only one personality type. The Enneagram goes further and makes it clear that everyone is a mixture of his or her basic type and *one* of the two types adjacent to it on the circumference of the Enneagram. This second type is called the *wing.*

The basic personality type accounts for many of the motivations and behaviors found in our overall personality, while the wing complements the basic type and adds important, sometimes contradictory, elements to it. The wing is our "second side," and must be taken into consideration to understand ourselves and others more insightfully. For example, a Nine will have either a One-wing or an Eight-wing, and can best be understood by considering the traits of the Nine uniquely blended with the traits of either the One or the Eight.

Strictly speaking, everyone's personality has elements from all nine types. This means that the type on the other side of your basic type also plays some part in your overall makeup. However, close observation and testing with the *Riso Enneagram Type*

Indicator reveals that everyone has a *dominant wing.* While the "second wing" remains operative to some lesser degree, the dominant wing is more important. For example, Twos with Three-wings are noticeably different from Twos with One-wings, and while Twos with Three-wings possess elements of type One, the Three-wing is more important and is dominant. It is more succinct to refer simply to a type's "wing" rather than its "dominant wing," since the two terms represent the same concept.

Directions of Integration and Disintegration

The nine personality types of the Enneagram are not static categories: they are open-ended and reflect our psychological growth and deterioration. The numbers on the Enneagram are connected in a sequence that denotes each personality type's Direction of Integration (health, self-actualization) and Direction of Disintegration (unhealth, neurosis). In other words, as individuals of each type become healthy or unhealthy, they change in different ways, as indicated and predicted by the lines of the Enneagram connected to their basic type.

The *Direction of Disintegration* for each type is indicated by the sequence of numbers 1-4-2-8-5-7-1. This means that if an unhealthy One deteriorates further, it will be to Four; an unhealthy Four will deteriorate to Two, an unhealthy Two will deteriorate to Eight, an unhealthy Eight to Five, an unhealthy Five to Seven, and an unhealthy Seven to One. (An easy way to remember the sequence is to realize that 1-4, or 14, doubles to 28, and that doubles to 57 — or almost so. Thus, 1-4-2-8-5-7 — the sequence returns to 1 and begins again.)

Likewise, on the equilateral triangle, the sequence is 9-6-3-9: an unhealthy Nine will deteriorate to Six, an unhealthy Six will deteriorate to Three, and an unhealthy Three will deteriorate to Nine. (You can remember this sequence if you think of the numerical values *diminishing* as the types become more unhealthy. For a longer explanation and examples, see *Personality Types,* 38–39.) You can see how this works by following the direction of the arrows on the following Enneagram.

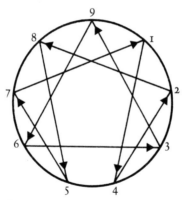

The Direction of Disintegration

1—4—2—8—5—7—1
9—6—3—9

The following brief descriptions will give you an idea of what happens to each type as it moves in its Direction of Disintegration. For more, see the full descriptions in *Personality Types.*

Unhealthy **Ones** become disillusioned with their ideals, finding that they can no longer hope to attain perfection; when they move toward Four, they become depressed and self-destructive.

Unhealthy **Fours** despair of ever actualizing themselves and their dreams in life; when they move toward Two, they can no longer function and become coercively dependent on others to take care of them.

Unhealthy **Twos** are highly resentful of the ungrateful treatment they feel they have gotten from others; when they move toward Eight, they strike out at those who have not responded to them in the way they have wanted.

Unhealthy **Eights** have dominated their environment so completely that they have made enemies of everyone around them; when they go toward Five, they become paranoid about their continued dominance, and possibly even their survival.

Unhealthy **Fives** have become isolated and incapable of acting effectively in their environment; when they go toward Seven, they begin to act impulsively and unpredictably.

Unhealthy **Sevens** have become manic and anxiously out of control of their thoughts and their actions; when they go toward One, they impose an arbitrary order in their life, becoming obsessive and compulsive.

Unhealthy **Nines** have become so dissociated and helpless that they can no longer function; when they go toward Six, they become abjectly self-defeating so that others will have to take care of them.

Unhealthy **Sixes** have become self-defeating and feel extremely inferior; when they go toward Three, they violently strike out at others both to overcome their inferiority feelings, and to hurt anyone who has hurt them.

Unhealthy **Threes** have become so consumed by their hostile feelings that they can no longer function in their environment; when they go toward Nine, they dissociate themselves from all of their feelings and shut down completely.

The *Direction of Integration* is indicated for each type by the *reverse* of the sequences for disintegration. Each type moves toward psychological integration in a direction that is the opposite of its unhealthy direction. The sequence for the Direction of Integration is 1-7-5-8-2-4-1. That is, an integrating One goes to Seven, an integrating Seven goes to Five, an integrating Five goes to Eight, an integrating Eight goes to Two, an integrating Two goes to Four, and an integrating Four goes to One. On the equilateral triangle, the sequence is 9-3-6-9: an integrating Nine will go to Three, an integrating Three will go to Six, and an integrating Six will go to Nine. You can see how this works by following the direction of the arrows on the following Enneagram.

The following brief descriptions will give you an idea of what happens to each type when it moves in its Direction of Integration. For more, see the full descriptions in *Personality Types*.

When balanced **Ones** go toward Seven, they accept reality with its necessary imperfections and become more productive; they no longer feel that they have to strive constantly to make everything perfect, and so relax and allow themselves to enjoy life.

When balanced **Sevens** go toward Five, they become involved with things in depth, contributing to their environment rather than merely consuming it; they no longer fear that they will be deprived of happiness if they are not constantly obtaining new

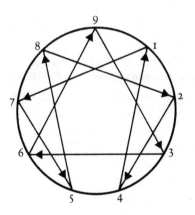

The Direction of Integration

1–7–5–8–2–4–1
9–3–6–9

things and experiences, and so are able to find more reliable sources of satisfaction.

When balanced **Fives** go toward Eight, they become courageous, acting from a realization of their own mastery; they feel that they have learned enough to act resourcefully and to lead others with self-confidence; they no longer fear that they will be overwhelmed by their environment, and so are able to meet challenges knowing that they can cope with whatever life brings.

When balanced **Eights** go toward Two, they become nurturing and helpful, concerned for the welfare of others instead of their own self-interest and aggrandizement; they no longer dominate the environment aggressively, and so are able to open to their own feelings and elicit love and devotion from others.

When balanced **Twos** go toward Four, they get in touch with their genuine feelings and motivations; they realize that they have legitimate needs which deserve to be fulfilled; they no longer feel that they have to be all-good and constantly of service to others, and so are able to be truly loved by being more authentic themselves.

When balanced **Fours** go toward One, they become self-disciplined and act on objective principles as well as subjective feelings; they no longer think of themselves as special, or feel the need to be self-indulgent or exempt in any way, and so are able to involve themselves actively in the world and discover who they truly are.

When balanced **Nines** go toward Three, they become more attentive, self-assured, and interested in developing themselves and their talents; they no longer feel that they have to live through someone else, and so they become their own person, bringing their considerable fortitude and strength of character to the world.

When balanced **Threes** go toward Six, they begin to identify with others, and find that by being steadfast and committed, they develop themselves more deeply; they are no longer competitive with anyone else, and so are able to support and inspire others while forming lasting, intimate relationships with them.

When balanced **Sixes** go toward Nine, they become accepting and supportive of others who are different from themselves, thus overcoming their own anxiety and negativity; they no longer feel that they have to prove themselves or defend themselves from anyone, and so can be more confident and positive about life.

It is unnecessary to have separate Enneagrams for the Directions of Integration and Disintegration. Both Directions can be shown on one Enneagram by eliminating the arrows and connecting the proper points with plain lines.

No matter which personality type you are, the types in *both* your Directions of Integration and Disintegration are important influences in your overall makeup. Thus, to obtain a complete picture of yourself (or of someone else), the basic type and wing as well as the two types in the Directions of Integration and Disintegration must be taken into consideration. The factors represented by these *four* types combine to produce your total personality and provide you with the framework for understanding the major psychological influences operating in you. For example, no one is simply a personality type Four. Fours have either a Three-wing or a Five-wing, and their Direction of Integration (One) and Direction of Disintegration (Two) also play important parts in their total personality and development. (For more details, see *Personality Types* and *Understanding the Enneagram*.)

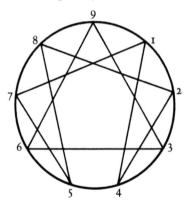

The Direction of Integration

1–7–5–8–2–4–1
9–3–6–9

The Direction of Disintegration

1–4–2–8–5–7–1
9–6–3–9

The Continuum of Traits

Within each personality type, there is an internal
structure. The Continuum (with its nine Levels of
Development) forms the backbone of each personality type. Understanding the Continuum and the
Levels of Development makes it clear that when we
change, we are shifting within the internal spectrum of motivations, traits, and defenses that make
up our type.

To understand a person accurately, it is necessary
to perceive where the person lies within the Levels
of his or her type. In other words, one must assess
whether a person is healthy, average, or unhealthy.
This is important because two people of the same
personality type and wing will differ significantly if
one is healthy and the other unhealthy. (In relationships and in Recovery, an understanding of this dis-
tinction is crucial.)

The Continuum for each of the personality types
is comprised of nine internal Levels of Development
and can be seen in the following diagram. Briefly,
there are three Levels in the healthy section, three
Levels in the average section, and three Levels in
the unhealthy section. It may help to think of the
Continuum as a photographer's gray scale, which
has gradations from pure white to pure black with
many shades of gray in between. On the Continuum, the healthiest traits appear first, at the top. As
one passes downward through each Level of Development, the Levels mark distinct shifts in deterio-

ration toward psychological breakdown. (In the Releases and Affirmations in this book, we reverse the order to follow the movement "upward" through the Levels of Development toward greater health and balance.)

The Continuum helps make sense of each personality type as a whole by providing a framework on which to place each healthy, average, and unhealthy trait, motivation, attitude, and defense mechanism. The Continuum is also worth understanding because it is in the healthy range that we are able to incorporate the behavior of the Direction of Integration, just as it is in the unhealthy range that we deteriorate more rapidly toward the Direction of

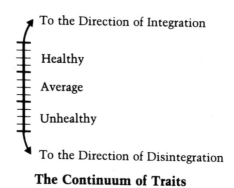

To the Direction of Integration

Healthy

Average

Unhealthy

To the Direction of Disintegration

The Continuum of Traits

Disintegration. The Enneagram corroborates the commonsense intuition that we must become healthy before we can integrate further, just as we must become somewhat unhealthy before we deteriorate into more negative and destructive states. We do not leap from neurosis to integration, or from health to instant neurosis. Integration, like disintegration, is a process that occurs over time. We can learn to be healthy just as, in different ways and for different reasons, we learn to be unhealthy. (For more information on this, see *Personality Types*, 41–2, 313–18; *Understanding the Enneagram*, 89–119.)

If we remember that the Enneagram is symbolic as well as psychological, we will understand that the personality types are metaphors for "functions" within ourselves (see *Discovering Your Personality Type*, 80–83). Each of the types symbolizes different aspects of what we need for wholeness and integration. The personality type into which we have developed early in life is less important than how we use our type as the starting point for self-development and self-transcendence.

We can also understand the Enneagram more dynamically: the "movements" around the Enneagram from type to type are metaphors for growth that results from the choices that we have made. The Enneagram predicts our development and our deterioration depending on the direction in which we move. If we move toward health, we will become more integrated, able to draw on the powers of each type for the development of our essence and spiritual capacities.

In the opposite direction, our personality disintegrates as we gradually lose the possibility of actualizing the capacities of our essence and spirit. This movement, in the Direction of Disintegration, is always easier and more enticing because it is truly "the path of least resistance," and is the result of giving in to the temptations and illusions of our personality. To climb the Levels of Development toward integration always requires a struggle against everything that draws us downward.

This is why self-observation is so important: we must know which actions and desires lead toward wholeness and which lead toward fragmentation. Self-observation provides us with the wisdom to make the right choices on our path. Without it, we would be lost.

Using the Transformations

People have found a variety of ways to incorporate these Transformations in their lives. Some have found it helpful to read them in the morning as part of their daily prayer or meditation, while others have found it useful to read them at night before going to sleep. Whenever you choose to read them, try to find a time when you will not be distracted and are receptive to what they evoke in you.

It is helpful to read the Transformations aloud, as this is an effective way of reprogramming your subconscious. With repetition, you will find that you may have memorized some of the Transformations and that they will spontaneously occur to you. You may want to hold an Affirmation or a Release in mind during stressful moments by repeating it several times in the manner of a prayer or mantra to shift your attention to something positive and helpful.

Remember to read the Transformations for the personality type of your wing. You may find that, in certain circumstances, the issues presented by your wing will be more significant to you than those of your basic type.

You may also want to read the Transformations

for the types in your Directions of Integration and Disintegration. The Affirmations of *healthy* attitudes and behavior of the type in your Direction of Integration can function as a beacon to illuminate your path toward growth. Conversely, the Releases of *unhealthy* attitudes and behavior for the type in your Direction of Disintegration can act as an "early warning signal," alerting you to aspects of yourself that may require more attention.

You will note that there are fewer positive Affirmations for each type than there are Releases of negative beliefs, feelings, and behavior. The positive Affirmations occupy only a third of each set of Transformations because there are nine Releases from the unhealthy Levels of Development and then seven Releases from the average Levels. Having worked through the Releases, we end on a positive note, in the nine Affirmations of the healthy Levels. Depending on your preferences, you may wish to read only the positive Affirmations most of the time, while reading the full set only occasionally.

The Forewords for each of the Transformations are meant to provide a brief summary of each type, with emphasis on how each gets into and out of its particular trap. The Forewords are not meant to be full descriptions of the types; for these, see *Personality Types*.

In my other books, I have offered a variety of profiles and detailed descriptions, as well as two questionnaires to help readers identify their personality type. Reading these Releases and Affirmations reflectively is an effective way to discover (or confirm) your personality type from yet another angle. The set of Transformations that touches you most deeply is probably that of your basic type. Moreover, the sets of Transformations for all nine personality types can be read by anyone regardless of his or her type since the Transformations reflect common human fears, motivations, and aspirations. We each contain all nine types, and so all the Transformations have something important to teach us about ourselves.

It is helpful to read the Transformations for the personality type of someone with whom you are having a misunderstanding, since doing so will enable you to get "inside" the other person's psyche for a more compassionate view of them. Understanding, and especially *feeling*, what it is like to be the other person may help you find creative solutions for conflicts.

The Transformations can also be used as informal checklists of the most important features of each type. Used this way, they can be helpful to parents and teachers, for example, in assessing the growth and development of those in their care. They will be able to evaluate whether or not children have developed the different psychological and emotional qualities touched on by the Transformations for their types; if not, the Transformations may be useful for determining what needs to be done to remedy the situation.

Each page of the Transformations has blank space

for composing your own Releases and Affirmations or to jot down the reactions and memories that the Transformations evoke. You may want to write down an incident, someone's name, or another association that helps you explore the Transformations and their implications more deeply.

The Transformations begin with personality type One, *The Reformer*, and proceed numerically to type Nine, *The Peacemaker*.

PART II

The Transformations

The Reformer

The Rational, Idealistic Type

REMEMBER THAT ONES TRY TO ESCAPE from their fear of being condemned by striving to be perfect. They see themselves as fair, reasonable, and objective, although others may see them as rigid, dogmatic, and overly critical. Ones believe that if they discipline themselves sufficiently, they can avoid making mistakes. Being human, however, they *do* make mistakes — obliging them to struggle ever harder to organize and improve everything in their lives. If they see that others do not share their idealism, Ones increasingly become unable to control their anger about having to do everything themselves. If Ones continue pushing themselves toward "perfection," the repressed parts of their psyches explode, leaving them enraged and irrational.

ONES CAN ESCAPE THEIR TRAP by acknowledging and releasing their unrealistic expectations of themselves and others. They begin to understand that the standards by which they judge the world are not absolute truths. As Ones recognize the subjective quality of many of their positions, they begin to respect the beliefs and values of others. Without the constraints of perfectionism, their vision opens to a reality more mysterious and more perfect than they could ever have conceived.

Transformations for
PERSONALITY TYPE ONE

1. I NOW RELEASE
   holding myself and others
   to impossible standards.

2. I NOW RELEASE
   my fear of losing control
   and becoming irrational.

3. I NOW RELEASE
   my fear of being condemned
   for being wrong.

4. I NOW RELEASE
   refusing to see my own
   contradictions.

5. I NOW RELEASE
   rationalizing my own behavior.

6. I NOW RELEASE
   obsessing about things I
   cannot change.

7.   I NOW RELEASE
     all bitterness and disappointment
     with the world.

8.   I NOW RELEASE
     feeling that other people's beliefs
     and values threaten mine.

9.   I NOW RELEASE
     believing that I am in a position
     to judge others.

10. I NOW RELEASE
    driving myself and others
    to be perfect.

11. I NOW RELEASE
    ignoring my own emotional
    and physical distress.

12. I NOW RELEASE
    feeling angry, impatient,
    and easily annoyed.

13. I NOW RELEASE
   fearing and disowning my body
   and my feelings.

14. I NOW RELEASE
   allowing my desire for order and
   efficiency to control my life.

15. I NOW RELEASE
   automatically focusing on
   what is wrong with things.

16. I NOW RELEASE
   feeling that it is up to me
   to fix everything.

17. I NOW AFFIRM
    that I can allow myself to relax
    and enjoy life.

18. I NOW AFFIRM
    that the best I can do
    is good enough.

19. I NOW AFFIRM
    that I am grateful that others
    have many things to teach me.

20. I NOW AFFIRM
    that I can make mistakes without
    condemning myself.

21. I NOW AFFIRM
    that my feelings are legitimate and
    that I have a right to feel them.

22. I NOW AFFIRM
    that I treat others with
    tenderness and respect.

23. I NOW AFFIRM
    that I am gentle and forgiving
    of myself.

24. I NOW AFFIRM
    that I am compassionate
    and forgiving of others.

25. I NOW AFFIRM
    that life is good and unfolding
    in miraculous ways.

PERSONALITY TYPE TWO:

The Helper
The Caring, Nurturing Type

REMEMBER THAT TWOS TRY TO ESCAPE their fear of being unloved by constantly doing things for others. They see themselves as thoughtful, well-meaning, and generous, although others may sometimes see them as intrusive and self-deceptive. To get others to love them, Twos believe that they must always be selfless and virtuous, so they sacrifice their own needs and desires for the good of others. If others still do not give Twos the love they want, their disappointment and anger must also be denied and repressed. Thus, Twos become caught between feeling love and feeling rage. Over time, suppressing their negative feelings takes its toll on their health and relationships and they lash out at the very people whose love they so desperately want.

TWOS CAN ESCAPE THEIR TRAP by acknowledging and releasing their ulterior motives and negative feelings toward others. The more honest they are about themselves, the more emotionally balanced they become. By recognizing and accepting all the different parts of themselves, even the negative ones, Twos undo the contradictions that have blocked them from being close to others. They can then become the genuinely loving, nurturing people they have always wanted to be. Their goodness is so real and selfless that they cannot help but attract others who love them deeply.

Transformations for
PERSONALITY TYPE TWO

1. **I NOW RELEASE**
   all feelings of rage and resentment
   toward others.

2. **I NOW RELEASE**
   all attempts to justify
   my aggressive feelings.

3. **I NOW RELEASE**
   all attachment to feeling
   victimized and abused.

4. I NOW RELEASE
the fear that I am unwanted
and unloved.

5. I NOW RELEASE
all attempts to force
others to love me.

6. I NOW RELEASE
making others feel guilty for not
responding sufficiently to my needs.

7. I NOW RELEASE
   abusing food and medications to
   make up for my loneliness.

8. I NOW RELEASE
   feeling that others owe me for the
   things I have chosen to do for them.

9. I NOW RELEASE
   believing that no one willingly
   takes care of me.

10. I NOW RELEASE
    expecting others to repay my help
    in the way *I* want.

11. I NOW RELEASE
    all physical ailments, aches,
    and complaints.

12. I NOW RELEASE
    calling attention to what I
    have done for others.

13. I NOW RELEASE
feeling possessive of loved ones.

14. I NOW RELEASE
doing things for others
to make myself needed.

15. I NOW RELEASE
flattering others to make them
feel good about me.

16. I NOW RELEASE
not wanting to acknowledge
my negative feelings.

17. I NOW AFFIRM
    that I own all of my feelings
    without fear.

18. I NOW AFFIRM
    that I am clear and conscious of
    my motives.

19. I NOW AFFIRM
    that I am lovable for
    who I am.

20. I NOW AFFIRM
    that my happiness does not depend
    on pleasing others.

21. I NOW AFFIRM
    that I can let go of loved ones.

22. I NOW AFFIRM
    that I nurture my own growth
    and development.

23.   I NOW AFFIRM
       that I love others without
       expecting anything in return.

24.   I NOW AFFIRM
       the joy and warmth that
       fills my heart.

25.   I NOW AFFIRM
       my gratitude for all that
       others have given me.

PERSONALITY TYPE THREE:

The Motivator

The Success-Oriented, Pragmatic Type

REMEMBER THAT THREES TRY TO ESCAPE from their fear of being rejected by seeking the affirmation of others through personal excellence. They see themselves as competent and worthwhile, although to others, they may seem attention-seeking and arrogant. If Threes sense that others are not responding to them, they begin to project an image that they believe will be more desirable. Thus, Threes disown their true self piece by piece and invest their energy in the roles they play until they lose touch with their feelings and any sense of who they really are. Terrified that someone will see through their facade to the growing emptiness inside, they may betray themselves and others to save their image.

THREES CAN ESCAPE THEIR TRAP by acknowledging and releasing their desire for attention and admiration. They see that their ceaseless search for applause alienates them from themselves and leads them away from deeper values. As they dare to give up their masks, they discover that they are not empty; they have many long-buried feelings and selfless impulses. And, by pursuing values and relationships that truly nourish their spirit, they discover that the authentic self they have so long concealed is more admirable than any image they could project.

1. I NOW RELEASE
   being obsessed by my hostile
   feelings toward others.

2. I NOW RELEASE
   believing that sabotaging others
   will make things better for me.

3. I NOW RELEASE
   feeling jealous of others and
   their good fortune.

4. I NOW RELEASE
   my fear of failing and
   being humiliated.

5. I NOW RELEASE
   fearing that I am inadequate
   and will be rejected.

6. I NOW RELEASE
   feeling that I must conceal
   my mistakes and limitations.

7. I NOW RELEASE
    closing down my feelings
    in order to function.

8. I NOW RELEASE
    betraying my own integrity to get
    the admiration of others.

9. I NOW RELEASE
    attempting to misrepresent myself
    and my abilities.

10. I NOW RELEASE
the grandiose expectations
I have of myself.

11. I NOW RELEASE
craving constant attention
and affirmation.

12. I NOW RELEASE
using arrogance to compensate
for my own insecurity.

13. I NOW RELEASE
     desiring to impress others
     with my performance.

14. I NOW RELEASE
     concealing myself behind masks.

15. I NOW RELEASE
     comparing myself with others.

16. I NOW RELEASE
     driving myself relentlessly
     to be the best.

17. I NOW AFFIRM
    that I have value regardless
    of my achievements.

18. I NOW AFFIRM
    that I am centered and
    emotionally available.

19. I NOW AFFIRM
    that I am caring
    and have a good heart.

20. I NOW AFFIRM
that I take in the love
others give me.

21. I NOW AFFIRM
that I am responsible to those
who look up to me.

22. I NOW AFFIRM
that I am happy to work
for the good of others.

23. I NOW AFFIRM
    that I develop my true talents by
    accepting who I am.

24. I NOW AFFIRM
    that I delight in the accomplishments
    and successes of others.

25. I NOW AFFIRM
    that I can reveal my real self
    without being afraid.

The Artist

The Sensitive, Withdrawn Type

REMEMBER THAT FOURS TRY TO ESCAPE from their fear of being flawed and defective by throwing themselves into their feelings. They see themselves as sensitive and intuitive, while others may see them as overly touchy and too ruled by their feelings. Fours believe that they will find a solution to their emotional turmoil by endlessly replaying their problems in their imaginations. As they go around and around, they stir up powerful emotional crosscurrents that draw them further inward until they lose all perspective on themselves, undermining their ability to deal effectively with life. In time, their emotional conflicts and difficulties fan the flames of their self-doubt and self-hatred, and they withdraw into a darkening world of torment and despair.

FOURS CAN ESCAPE THEIR TRAP by acknowledging and releasing their strong attachments to their feelings. As they do so, Fours learn that their feelings do not die, as they had feared, but that other capacities and talents become available and can be acted on. The more they interact with reality, the richer their emotional life becomes. No longer the prisoners of every shifting mood, they find that their practical accomplishments grow. Fours thus discover that they are not only intuitive and creative, but also capable and strong.

Transformations for
PERSONALITY TYPE FOUR

1. I NOW RELEASE
   turning my anger and aggressions
   against myself.

2. I NOW RELEASE
   all self-hatred and self-contempt.

3. I NOW RELEASE
   all feelings of hopelessness
   and despair.

4. I NOW RELEASE
   all self-sabotaging thoughts
   and actions.

5. I NOW RELEASE
   feeling that I am inadequate
   and defective.

6. I NOW RELEASE
   the fear that I am unimportant
   and undesirable.

7. I NOW RELEASE
feeling shameful and misunderstood
by others.

8. I NOW RELEASE
being distraught, fatigued,
and inhibited.

9. I NOW RELEASE
feeling that people always
let me down.

10. I NOW RELEASE
     all unrealistic expectations
     of myself and others.

11. I NOW RELEASE
     all claims of needing to be
     treated differently.

12. I NOW RELEASE
     all self-indulgence in my
     emotions and behavior.

13. I NOW RELEASE
all self-doubt and emotional
vulnerability.

14. I NOW RELEASE
wanting to protect myself by
withdrawing from others.

15. I NOW RELEASE
all wasteful fantasies and
romantic longings.

16. I NOW RELEASE
dwelling on the past
to prolong my feelings.

17.   I NOW AFFIRM
      that I am not defined
      by my feelings.

18.   I NOW AFFIRM
      that only the feelings I act on
      express who I am.

19.   I NOW AFFIRM
      that I open myself up to people
      and the world.

20. **I NOW AFFIRM**
     that I use all of my
     experiences to grow.

21. **I NOW AFFIRM**
     the goodness of my life,
     my friends, and myself.

22. **I NOW AFFIRM**
     that I love myself and
     treat myself gently.

23. I NOW AFFIRM
     that I am free of the damage
     of my past.

24. I NOW AFFIRM
     that I am transforming my life
     into something higher.

25. I NOW AFFIRM
     that I am bringing something good
     and beautiful into the world.

PERSONALITY TYPE FIVE:

The Thinker

The Intellectual, Analytic Type

REMEMBER THAT FIVES TRY TO ESCAPE from their fear of being overwhelmed and powerless by focusing on specific areas of life which they feel they can master. They see themselves as intelligent and profound, although others may see them as too intense and strangely detached. As Fives become convinced that they cannot cope with people or with practical life, they retreat into private mental worlds. They seek sanctuary in their minds while watching the outside world with growing anxiety. Eventually, their fears taint their thoughts so much that Fives feel they must cut off their connections with the world to protect themselves from their terrors. With nothing to hold on to or believe in, they ultimately shrink away into a self-created prison of isolation and hopelessness.

FIVES CAN ESCAPE THEIR TRAP by acknowledging and releasing their fears of being powerless and overwhelmed by the outside world. By disengaging from their overheated mental associations, Fives discover that in the present moment, they can indeed be safe and at ease in the environment. They begin to focus on those things that support them rather than threaten them. As they leave their shell, Fives realize not only that there is a place for them in the world, but that they are capable of enjoying and mastering life.

Transformations for
PERSONALITY TYPE FIVE

1. **I NOW RELEASE**
   all fearfulness of the world
   around me.

2. **I NOW RELEASE**
   all feelings of powerlessness
   and hopelessness.

3. **I NOW RELEASE**
   my fear of being violated
   or overwhelmed by others.

4. I NOW RELEASE
   my dark and destructive fantasies.

5. I NOW RELEASE
   isolating myself by
   rejecting others.

6. I NOW RELEASE
   believing that no one can
   be depended on.

7. I NOW RELEASE
   desiring to antagonize others
   and ruin their peace of mind.

8. I NOW RELEASE
   being cynical and contemptuous of the
   normalcy of others.

9. I NOW RELEASE
   fearing that others will
   exploit me.

10. I NOW RELEASE
feeling that I am a
misfit in life.

11. I NOW RELEASE
being secretive and hiding
from people.

12. I NOW RELEASE
postponing my emotional needs.

13. I NOW RELEASE
neglecting my physical health
and appearance.

14. I NOW RELEASE
the agitation and restlessness
of my mind.

15. I NOW RELEASE
feeling that I always need to know
more before I do anything.

16. I NOW RELEASE
avoiding my life by escaping
into my mind.

17.   I NOW AFFIRM
      that I am secure and grounded in
      the reality of my own life.

18.   I NOW AFFIRM
      the strength and wonder
      of my body.

19.   I NOW AFFIRM
      the value of my inventiveness
      and sense of humor.

20. I NOW AFFIRM
    that I accept uncertainty
    and ambiguity.

21. I NOW AFFIRM
    that my life and struggles are
    meaningful and rewarding.

22. I NOW AFFIRM
    that I have faith in the future
    and in human beings.

23. I NOW AFFIRM
that I reach out to others
confidently as an equal.

24. I NOW AFFIRM
that I find serenity in being
compassionate toward others.

25. I NOW AFFIRM
that I support others from the
fullness of my heart.

The Loyalist

The Committed, Traditionalistic Type

REMEMBER THAT SIXES TRY TO ESCAPE from their fear of being abandoned by allying themselves with others. They see themselves as trustworthy and reliable, although others may see them as defensive and insecure. They want to feel that they belong somewhere, so they look to others to provide security and show them what to do. The problem is that Sixes are also anxious about depending on others. They are thus caught between needing the security of an authority and wanting to prove their independence. Sixes may try to solve their anxiety with outbursts of misdirected aggression against those around them. When their outbursts drive away supporters and protectors, Sixes become all the more anxious and depressed.

SIXES CAN ESCAPE THEIR TRAP by acknowledging and releasing their feelings of dependency. By learning to center themselves and trust their own capacities, they find a stable place within themselves. They learn that they can believe in themselves, and that they do not need to depend on others to "save" them. They stop relinquishing their authority to others and take constructive actions for their own welfare. When Sixes dare to pursue their *own* values and beliefs, they begin to discover the real courage and security they have always sought.

Transformations for
PERSONALITY TYPE SIX

1. **I NOW RELEASE**
   my fear of being abandoned
   and alone.

2. **I NOW RELEASE**
   my self-defeating, self-punishing
   tendencies.

3. **I NOW RELEASE**
   all feelings of dread
   about the future.

4. I NOW RELEASE
    feeling persecuted, trapped,
    and desperate.

5. I NOW RELEASE
    overreacting and exaggerating
    my problems.

6. I NOW RELEASE
    taking out my fears and
    anxieties on others.

7. I NOW RELEASE
   being suspicious of others and
   thinking the worst of them.

8. I NOW RELEASE
   feeling inferior and incapable
   of functioning on my own.

9. I NOW RELEASE
   feeling cowardly and unsure
   of myself.

10. I NOW RELEASE
     acting "tough" to disguise
     my insecurities.

11. I NOW RELEASE
     my fear and dislike of those who
     are different from me.

12. I NOW RELEASE
     blaming others for my own
     problems and mistakes.

13. I NOW RELEASE
    being evasive and defensive
    with those who need me.

14. I NOW RELEASE
    my tendency to be negative
    and complaining.

15. I NOW RELEASE
    my fear of taking responsibility
    for my mistakes.

16. I NOW RELEASE
    looking to others to make me
    feel secure.

17. I NOW AFFIRM
     that I am independent
     and capable.

18. I NOW AFFIRM
     that I can keep my own identity
     in groups and in relationships.

19. I NOW AFFIRM
     that I have faith in myself,
     my talents, and my future.

20. I NOW AFFIRM
    that I meet difficulties
    with calmness and confidence.

21. I NOW AFFIRM
    that I am secure and able to make
    the best of whatever comes my way.

22. I NOW AFFIRM
    the kinship I have with every
    human being.

23. I NOW AFFIRM
    that I am understanding and generous
    to all who need me.

24. I NOW AFFIRM
    that I act courageously in
    all circumstances.

25. I NOW AFFIRM
    that I find true authority
    within me.

The Generalist

The Hyperactive, Uninhibited Type

REMEMBER THAT SEVENS TRY TO ESCAPE from their fear of being deprived by immersing themselves in constant activity. They see themselves as practical and fun-loving, although others may see them as superficial and infantile. Sevens fear that if they run out of stimulation — of things to have and do — something terrible will happen, so they stay busy and on the go. They spread themselves too thin, however, using up their resources, while constantly distracting themselves with even more experiences. Eventually, the strain causes their health and emotional stability to collapse, and Sevens are left exhausted and in panic.

SEVENS CAN ESCAPE THEIR TRAP by acknowledging and releasing their attachment to being stimulated all the time. When they slow down, they discover that many of their activities do not actually satisfy them. And, as they let go of their feeling that they must be constantly having new experiences, they learn to stay with each experience long enough to assimilate it. Sevens finally realize that no experience or thing in the external world can ultimately keep them satisfied or free from anxiety, but if they search within themselves, they will find a stillness and serenity which is a dependable source of undiminished joy.

Transformations for
PERSONALITY TYPE SEVEN

1. **I NOW RELEASE**
    all reckless and destructive
    impulses.

2. **I NOW RELEASE**
    feeling that I will be
    overwhelmed by anxiety.

3. **I NOW RELEASE**
    all compulsions and addictions.

4. I NOW RELEASE
   burning myself out by trying to
   satisfy all of my desires.

5. I NOW RELEASE
   running away from the consequences
   of my actions.

6. I NOW RELEASE
   insulting or abusing others
   to vent my frustrations.

7. **I NOW RELEASE**
   allowing my insecurities to drive me
   into dangerous situations and behavior.

8. **I NOW RELEASE**
   sacrificing my health and happiness
   for instant gratification.

9. **I NOW RELEASE**
   being demanding and impatient
   with others.

10. I NOW RELEASE
    fearing that there will not be
    enough for me.

11. I NOW RELEASE
    always feeling that I need more.

12. I NOW RELEASE
    wanting every moment to be
    exciting and dramatic.

13. I NOW RELEASE
escaping from myself through
distractions and constant activity.

14. I NOW RELEASE
letting my lack of self-discipline
ruin my opportunities.

15. I NOW RELEASE
overextending myself with more
than I can do well.

16. I NOW RELEASE
believing that external things
will make me happy.

17. I NOW AFFIRM
     that I am happiest when I am
     calm and centered.

18. I NOW AFFIRM
     that I can say no to myself
     without feeling deprived.

19. I NOW AFFIRM
     that there will be enough for me
     of whatever I need.

20. I NOW AFFIRM
     that I am resilient in the face
     of setbacks.

21. I NOW AFFIRM
     that I find satisfaction in
     ordinary things.

22. I NOW AFFIRM
     that I stay with projects until
     I complete them.

23. I NOW AFFIRM
    that I care deeply about people and
    am committed to their happiness.

24. I NOW AFFIRM
    that there is a spiritual dimension
    to my life.

25. I NOW AFFIRM
    that I am profoundly grateful
    to be alive.

The Leader

The Powerful, Dominating Type

REMEMBER THAT EIGHTS TRY TO ESCAPE from their fear of being in the power or control of others by maintaining a stance of strength and toughness. They see themselves as strong and independent, although others may see them as belligerent and dictatorial. In their effort to suppress their fear and vulnerability, Eights begin to see all relationships as power struggles and all intimacy as weakness. They steel themselves against depending on others, and seek more power so that no one can take advantage of them. If they continue hardening themselves, they eventually lose the capacity to feel anything for others — love, trust, or pity. Eights ultimately become abusive to get their way and remain in control, causing everyone who has been abused by them to turn against them.

EIGHTS CAN ESCAPE THEIR TRAP by acknowledging and releasing their fear of intimacy. As they do so, they begin to drop their guard and discover that real love and friendship will not threaten them. They find that the more they trust and care for others, the more others willingly support them and help them attain their goals. By allowing others to be close to them, Eights are able to create a world of cooperation and mutual fulfillment rather than one of conflict and mutual destruction.

Transformations for
PERSONALITY TYPE EIGHT

1. **I NOW RELEASE**
   all anger, rage, and violence
   from my life.

2. **I NOW RELEASE**
   dehumanizing myself by violating
   others in any way.

3. **I NOW RELEASE**
   being verbally or physically abusive.

4. I NOW RELEASE
believing that taking vengeance will
free me from my own pain.

5. I NOW RELEASE
hardening my heart
against suffering.

6. I NOW RELEASE
my fear of ever being vulnerable
or weak.

7. I NOW RELEASE
   believing that I do not
   need others.

8. I NOW RELEASE
   believing that I must bully
   people to get my way.

9. I NOW RELEASE
   my fear that others will
   control me.

10.   I NOW RELEASE
        feeling that I must only
        look after myself.

11.   I NOW RELEASE
        my fear of losing to anyone.

12.   I NOW RELEASE
        feeling that I must
        never be afraid.

1 3 .   I NOW RELEASE
attempting to control everything
in my life.

1 4 .   I NOW RELEASE
allowing my pride and ego to ruin
my health and relationships.

1 5 .   I NOW RELEASE
thinking that anyone who does not
agree with me is against me.

1 6 .   I NOW RELEASE
being hard-boiled and denying
my need for affection.

17. I NOW AFFIRM
    that I believe in people and care
    about their welfare.

18. I NOW AFFIRM
    that I am big-hearted and let
    others share the glory.

19. I NOW AFFIRM
    that I am honorable and therefore
    worthy of respect.

20. I NOW AFFIRM
    that I am most fulfilled by
    championing others.

21. I NOW AFFIRM
    that I have tender feelings
    and good impulses.

22. I NOW AFFIRM
    that I can be gentle without
    being afraid.

23. I NOW AFFIRM
     that I master myself and my own
     passions.

24. I NOW AFFIRM
     that there is an authority greater
     than me.

25. I NOW AFFIRM
     that I love others and ask for
     their love in return.

The Peacemaker

The Easygoing, Phlegmatic Type

REMEMBER THAT NINES TRY TO ESCAPE their fear of separation by creating an "environment" that will nurture them. They see themselves as undemanding, uncomplicated people, although others may feel that they are complacent and neglectful. Nines believe that everything should always be peaceful and harmonious. They begin to create problems, however, because they refuse to look at anything that contradicts their idealized world view, hoping for the best while ignoring difficulties until others are forced to solve them. Eventually, others become frustrated and angry with them, causing Nines to retreat into a psychic inner sanctum where nothing can touch or hurt them. They eventually turn their backs on reality and drift into a state of apathy and helplessness.

NINES CAN ESCAPE THEIR TRAP by acknowledging and releasing their idealizations of the world and others. As they do so, Nines see their loved ones more objectively and realize that others' lives are not inherently more important than their own. This frees Nines to see their own value and gives them the energy to become actively engaged with life. By investing in their own development, and participating fully in their world, Nines find the contentment they have always sought.

Transformations for
PERSONALITY TYPE NINE

1. I NOW RELEASE
not taking an active interest
in my own life.

2. I NOW RELEASE
turning away from whatever is
unpleasant or difficult.

3. I NOW RELEASE
feeling that there is nothing I can
do to improve my life.

4. I NOW RELEASE
   being numb and emotionally
   unavailable.

5. I NOW RELEASE
   refusing to see my
   own aggressions.

6. I NOW RELEASE
   ignoring problems until they
   become overwhelming.

7. I NOW RELEASE
   all dependency and fear of being
   on my own.

8. I NOW RELEASE
   all wishful thinking and giving up
   too soon.

9. I NOW RELEASE
   neglecting myself and my own
   legitimate needs.

10. I NOW RELEASE
seeking quick, easy "solutions"
to my problems.

11. I NOW RELEASE
feeling threatened by significant
changes in my life.

12. I NOW RELEASE
losing myself in comforting habits
and routines.

13. I NOW RELEASE
     feeling that most things are just
     too much trouble.

14. I NOW RELEASE
     all inattentiveness and
     forgetfulness.

15. I NOW RELEASE
     going along with others
     to keep the peace.

16. I NOW RELEASE
     living through others and not
     developing myself.

17. I NOW AFFIRM
    that I am confident, strong,
    and independent.

18. I NOW AFFIRM
    that I develop my mind and
    think things through.

19. I NOW AFFIRM
    that I am awake and alert to
    the world around me.

20. I NOW AFFIRM
that I am proud of myself
and my abilities.

21. I NOW AFFIRM
that I am steadfast and dependable
in difficult times.

22. I NOW AFFIRM
that I look deeply into myself
without fear.

23. I NOW AFFIRM
that I am excited about
my future.

24. I NOW AFFIRM
that I am a powerful, healing
force in my world.

25. I NOW AFFIRM
that I actively embrace all
that life brings.

PART III

Toward the Center

General Affirmations

WE FORGET WHAT WE NEED TO REMEMBER, and remember what we need to forget. It seems to be part of the human condition to need to be reminded again and again of the most important lessons of life — not because these lessons are so difficult to understand but because they are difficult for us to act on. We are such creatures of habit that it is difficult for us to remember anything beyond our recurring impulses, dreams, and desires. If we were able to do so, our lives would change quickly. If we were not so completely consumed by the tyranny of our fantasies, our values would shift and we would become different.

THERE IS A BETTER WAY TO DEVELOP, not by forcing ourselves into piecemeal changes, but by achieving a new state of being. We can change if we really want to, and these General Affirmations are reminders of some of the "right actions" we can take. Actions, however, are not enough: we must desire what is really good for us, and to do that, we must love ourselves. To love ourselves, we must remember to ask who we really are. This is the fundamental question that we constantly forget to ask, and the answer to which we need constantly to seek. These ever-shifting tides — remembering ourselves and forgetting ourselves, opening up and closing down, struggling higher and slipping lower, awakening and falling asleep — are not only the movements of our lives, but are the very rhythms of the Enneagram.

General Affirmations

1. **I NOW AFFIRM**
   that, from now on, I choose
   to live a better life.

2. **I NOW AFFIRM**
   that I learn from everyone
   and everything.

3. **I NOW AFFIRM**
   that I use the difficulties life
   brings to grow.

4. I NOW AFFIRM
that this day is precious, and I will
live it as if it were my last.

5. I NOW AFFIRM
that I choose to be effective
and productive.

6. I NOW AFFIRM
that I respect myself and care
properly for my body.

7. I NOW AFFIRM
   the health and energy of every part
   of my body.

8. I NOW AFFIRM
   that a joyful and bountiful life
   is my birthright.

9. I NOW AFFIRM
   that I observe myself
   without judgment.

10. I NOW AFFIRM
    that I will meditate or pray daily
    to center myself and remind myself
    of deeper values.

11. I NOW AFFIRM
    that I love myself and will do only
    what is truly good for me.

12. I NOW AFFIRM
    that I am courageous despite
    my fears.

13. **I NOW AFFIRM**
that my presence is significant
to the world.

14. **I NOW AFFIRM**
that I respect the integrity of others
while maintaining my own.

15. **I NOW AFFIRM**
that my words and deeds will only
be used to support and nourish others.

16. I NOW AFFIRM
    that I dedicate myself to nurturing
    those people and things that have
    been entrusted to my care.

17. I NOW AFFIRM
    that I forgive those who have
    wronged me.

18. I NOW AFFIRM
    that I seek forgiveness for the
    wrongs I have done.

19. I NOW AFFIRM
that I accept my mother and my father
for who they are and do not condemn
them for their failings.

20. I NOW AFFIRM
that I let go of all negative
thoughts, words, and actions.

21. I NOW AFFIRM
that I let go of the past and
open up to the present.

22.   I NOW AFFIRM
      that here, in this moment,
      all is well.

23.   I NOW AFFIRM
      the miracle of my own existence.

24.   I NOW AFFIRM
      that I act only on those desires that
      bring me closer to my Higher Power.

25.   I NOW AFFIRM
      that I cooperate with grace.

The Enneagram and Healing

And we are put on earth a little space,
that we may learn to bear the beams of love.
— William Blake

Learning to "bear the beams of love" is one of the most difficult things we can do. The problem is that we do not really understand love, its demands or tremendous power — much less how to bear it. On the contrary, we persuade ourselves that we would be supremely happy if we had even more love. We each think *we* would be the exception since *we* know what love is about. We long for love, we sentimentalize it, romanticize it, and lose ourselves in it. But real love is difficult to bear because we cannot turn it into something superficial. This deeper love penetrates to the very core of our being, beyond the part of us that protects (and unwittingly prolongs) the damage from our past.

No matter how fortunate we may have been in childhood, each of us has been damaged. One of the facts of human existence is that no one escapes childhood without having been deformed in some way. The necessity of finding a way of "fitting" into the circumstances of our lives means that some parts of us must be sacrificed. For some, the damage has resulted in learning to forget themselves, for others, it means hiding who they are, for others, it has required that they serve other people's needs rather than their own, for others, damage manifests itself in overcompensations of various sorts. The shared tragedy of our childhoods is that no type leaves it balanced or unscathed. Moreover, there is another cost which we pay again and again throughout our lives: the need to cover up our damage lest our wounds stay open and never heal.

Or so it seems to us. We feel the need to protect our wounded core from any further hurt, so our personality has formed a shell around our innermost self. Such beams of love as come our way are deflected by our personality or are snatched away by the wrong parts of it. The healing love we so desperately need cannot penetrate deeply enough to do us any good. To change this, we need to see that we will never bear the beams of love — and thus be healed — unless we get our personality out of the way.

Each personality type is thus an unwitting strategy for escaping from inner pain by pretending it is not there, by compensating for it in dangerous and destructive ways, by turning to others to solve it, or by being driven by it so relentlessly that we burn ourselves out rather than experience it directly. The further tragedy is that we become strangers to ourselves because we live in flight from who we are — or more precisely, from the shamed and damaged part of ourselves. Because we want nothing to do with our pain, we turn from it and create an identity out of the ways by which we stay in flight. Our style of escape becomes our personality type, and the Enneagram shows us what those methods of attempted escape are. Rather than merely acknowledge our type, however, we must force ourselves to look inward and heal our pain by understanding that "the way out is through." The pain at the core of each personality type must be touched if healing is to take place — not because we wish to suffer but because the pain needs to be healed so that our suffering can cease.

Miraculously, healing comes rapidly if our pain is acknowledged and experienced directly. By looking at ourselves as we are, not with comforting sentiment or gratuitous self-forgiveness but with unsparing honesty, we can become compassionate toward ourselves. The beams of love we need to learn to bear come from a higher part of ourselves that sees our suffering and is able to heal it.

What we need for healing is therefore simple, and always within our reach, because it comes both from and through that part of us that has not been damaged and is not in pain. Because we do not understand this, we try to bury and soothe our pain in futile ways. Unfortunately, these attempts are as useless as applying the wrong medicine to a wound: a hundred inappropriate bromides cannot produce what the proper remedy can.

If we were able to be present to ourselves, we would find the solution to our suffering. We would see that healing happens when we give names to the sources of our pain and let them go. When this takes place, we discover that a moment of "opening up and letting go" cures years of closing off and holding on.

The Recovery Movement teaches us that we must learn to reparent ourselves because only we can undo the damage of our childhood. While it is impossible to heal our past alone, it is also impossible to be healed by someone else. As unfair as it may seem, we must assume the burden of reparenting ourselves: after all, only we have been through the experience of our childhood, so only we are in a position to reclaim it.

We do this by finding the love for our self that our parents were unable to give. We must find compassion for that wounded part of ourselves that has endured so many difficulties and yet has still survived. The methods for getting by in childhood served us well in their day; now the time has come to let go of them and move on. Our need to withdraw from others, or to detach emotionally from those around us, to become untrusting and suspicious, to abandon ourselves to please people, or to use dozens of other strategies to make us feel secure will come to an end the day we start nurturing our own, true inner life.

One of the most important features of Twelve Step Programs is the requirement that people make a "fearless moral inventory" of their characters. The Transformations can help us with the difficult process of examining ourselves with complete honesty. Naturally, everyone is intimidated about looking at their character defects and emotional "issues." Most of us do not know where to begin to make an inventory of ourselves. Since we have probably come from families where we were criticized and shamed, it is easy to feel afraid that the negative things we find are not only true, but that they are the whole picture. If we fear that we cannot ever really change, it is all too easy to become discouraged and to sink into confusion and apathy.

There is something profoundly liberating, however, about realizing that most of our flaws and conflicts are not unique to us. While they may be deep, they are, in another sense, not our own. The worst aspects of our personality are also those of others: our defects are the common bondage of our type. Once we see how much we have in common with others of our type, we can identify with our deeper self instead of the more superficial aspects of our personality. In this sense, our failures are less a measure of our own defectiveness than the mark of a soul in pain crying out through the distorted mask of personality.

In the last analysis, *the Enneagram is about self-transformation through self-transcendence.* It shows us that we can be transformed if we stop identifying with our personality. We must risk creating an "opening" in ourselves that will allow something higher and more essential to touch our wounded self and heal it. These Releases and Affirmations are offered with the hope that they help you on your journey of inner healing. They are not the whole picture, of course — just a place to begin. Always remember, however, that when the shadows in ourselves are touched by the light of awareness, they become doors through which grace transforms our lives.

Your local bookstore can provide you with copies of all of Don Richard Riso's books: *Personality Types* (1987), *Understanding the Enneagram* (1990), *Discovering Your Personality Type: The Enneagram Questionnaire* (1992), and *Enneagram Transformations* (1993). Or you can order them from the publisher by calling (800) 225-3362.

To obtain multiple copies for use in Enneagram Workshops as well as business and organizational settings, please contact Houghton Mifflin Company, Special Sales Department, 215 Park Avenue South, New York, New York 10003, or phone (212) 420-5890. Special discounts are available for orders of ten copies or more.

To contact Don Richard Riso for information about his Enneagram Workshops, professional trainings, new publications, and business seminars, or to have your name added to his mailing list for Workshops in your area, please contact Enneagram Personality Types, Inc., at the address below.

For personal consulting or to have the *Riso Enneagram Type Indicator* interpreted by an Enneagram teacher trained and certified by Don Richard Riso, please contact Enneagram Personality Types, Inc., for a referral to a teacher in your area.

For a free brochure of Enneagram Designs products, call (800) 852-9704. Outside the United States, call (803) 548-1110.

Enneagram Personality Types, Inc.
222 Riverside Drive, Suite 10E
New York, N.Y. 10025
(212) 932-3306